PIANO / VOCAL HIGHLIGHTS

THE PRODUCERS

the new MEL BROOKS musical

BOOK BY
MEL BROOKS AND THOMAS MEEHAN

MUSIC AND LYRICS BY
MEL BROOKS

Original Broadway Cast Recording available on Sony Classical

Front Cover Photo: Norman Jean Roy

ISBN 0-634-05378-7

HAL•LEONARD®
CORPORATION
7777 W. BLUEMOUND RD. P.O. BOX 13819 MILWAUKEE, WI 53213

In Australia Contact:

Hal Leonard Australia Pty. Ltd.
22 Taunton Drive P.O. Box 5130
Cheltenham East, 3192 Victoria, Australia
Email: ausadmin@halleonard.com

Visit Hal Leonard Online at
www.halleonard.com

THE KING OF BROADWAY

Music and Lyrics by
MEL BROOKS

Fast 4 ♩ = 156

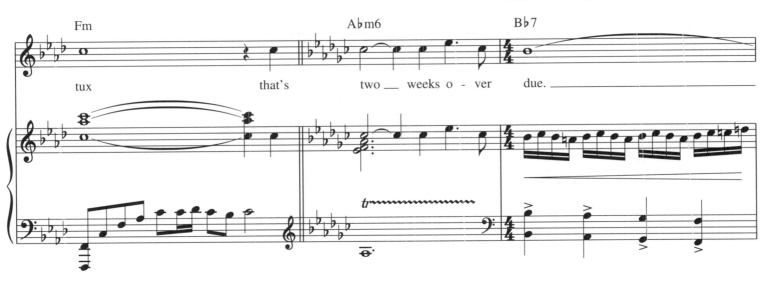

tux   that's   two __ weeks o - ver   due. _____

CHORUS:

Poor Bi - al - ly,   what a schmoo-zer,   poor Bi - al - y,   what a shame.

_____   Rent - ed __ tux _____   o - ver

Poor Bi - al - ly,   what a lo - ser,   poor Bi - al - ly,   Good-bye fame!

due _____   way o - ver due   I

WE CAN DO IT

Music and Lyrics by
MEL BROOKS

MAX:
What did Lew-is say to Clark when ev-'ry-thing looked bleak?

What did Sir Ed-mund say to Ten-zing as they strug-gled t'ward Ev-er-est's peak?

What did Wash-ing-ton say to his troops be - fore they crossed the Del-a-ware? _

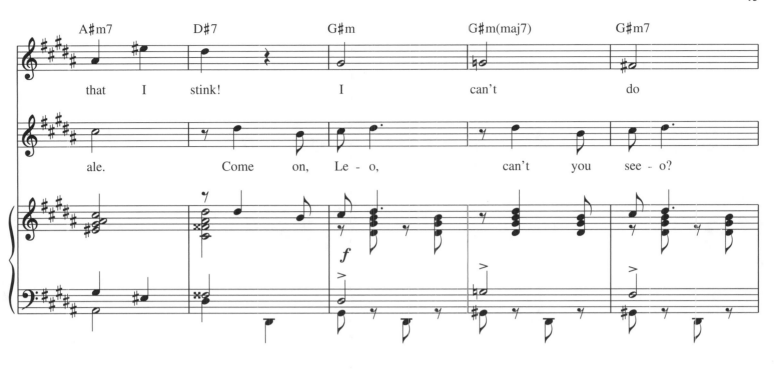

that I stink! I can't do ale. Come on, Le - o, can't you see - o?

LEO:

it. You see Ri - o, I see jail.

Ow!

MAX:

We can do it,

I WANNA BE A PRODUCER

Music and Lyrics by
MEL BROOKS

DER GUTEN TAG HOP-CLOP

Music and Lyrics by
MEL BROOKS

KEEP IT GAY

Music and Lyrics by
MEL BROOKS

Lightly, moderately slow

The thea-ter's so ob-sessed with dra-mas so de-pressed, it's

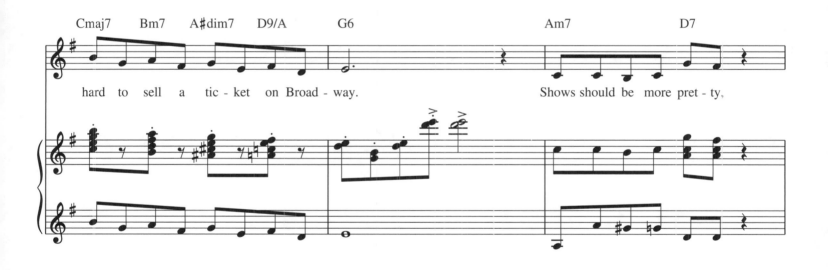

hard to sell a tic - ket on Broad - way. Shows should be more pret - ty,

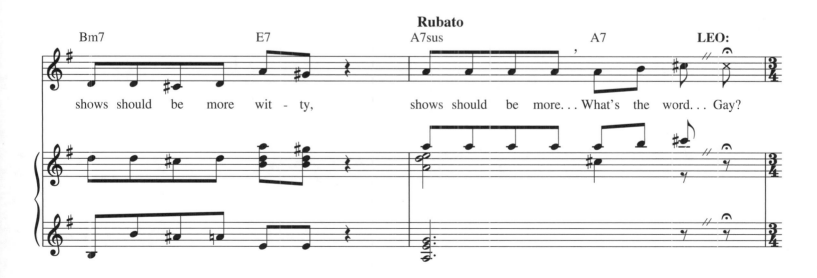

shows should be more wit - ty, shows should be more... What's the word... Gay?

WHEN YOU GOT IT, FLAUNT IT

Music and Lyrics by
MEL BROOKS

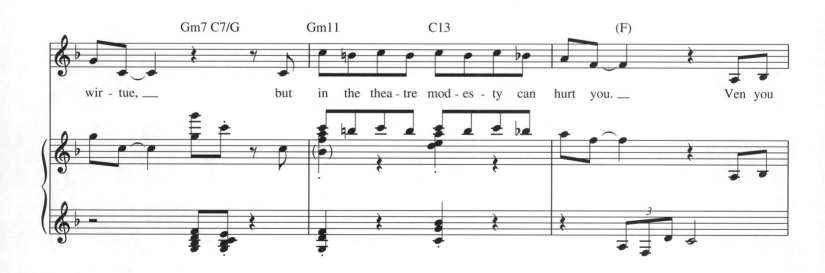

42

ALONG CAME BIALY

Music and Lyrics by
MEL BROOKS

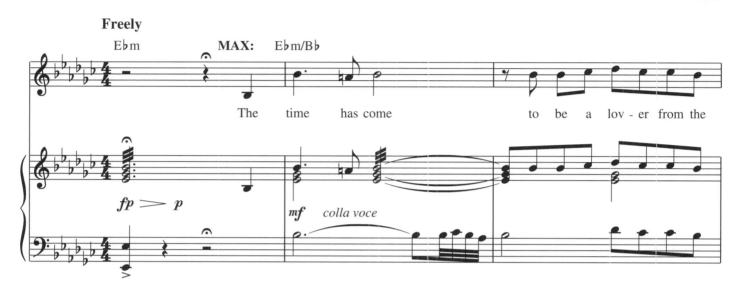

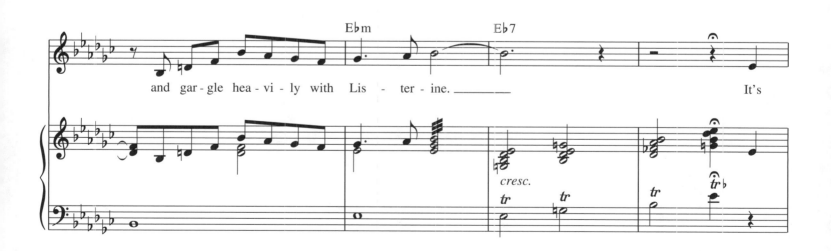

Lyrics:
The time has come to be a lov-er from the Ar-gen-tine, to slick my hair down with Bril-lian-tine, and gar-gle hea-vi-ly with Lis-ter-ine. It's

time for Max to put his back - ers on their backs

and thrill them with a - maz - ing acts, those a - ging nym - pho - ma - ni -

Tango

acs. Ah! _____ Ah! _____

They were help - less, _ they were hope - less _ then a long came Bi -

THAT FACE

Music and Lyrics by
MEL BROOKS

HABEN SIE GEHÖRT
DAS DEUTSCHE BAND?
(Have You Ever Heard the German Band?)

Music and Lyrics by
MEL BROOKS

SPRINGTIME FOR HITLER

Music and Lyrics by
MEL BROOKS

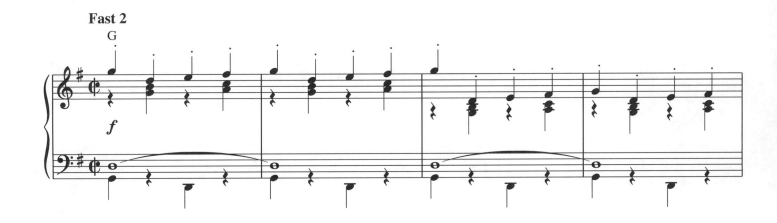

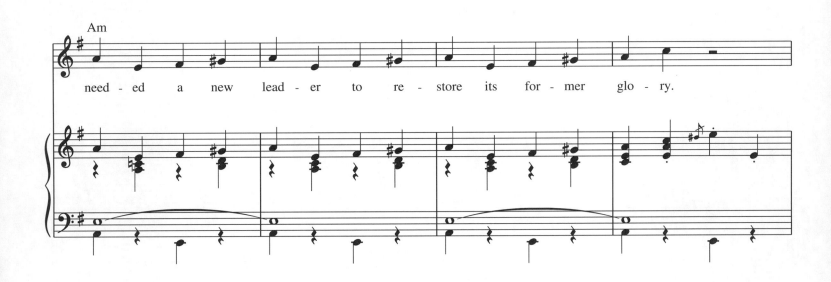

Where, oh where, was he? Where could that man be? We

STORM TROOPER:

looked a - round and then we found the man for you and me. And now it's

With a Lilt, in 4

Spring - time for Hit - ler and Ger - ma - ny,

Deutsch - land is hap - py and gay. _____

A Tempo

Spring-time for Hit-ler and Ger-ma-ny, ___

Goose-steps, the new step to-day. ___

Bombs fall-ing from the skies a-gain.

Bomb dropping

HEIL MYSELF

Music and Lyrics by
MEL BROOKS

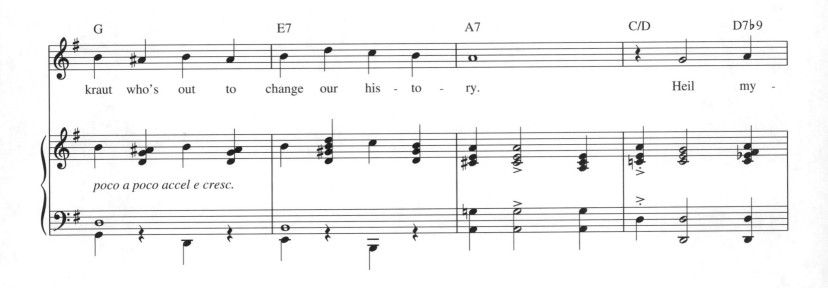

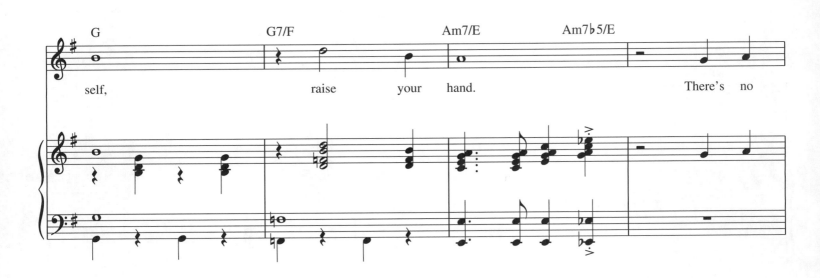

*Until noted, the downstemmed male notes sound as written (normally, these notes would appear an octave higher)

*Normal male voice notation

*traditional unison, males sing 8vb

*Male notes as written (normally would appear an octave higher)

BETRAYED

Music and Lyrics by
MEL BROOKS

Just like Cain and A - bel you pulled a sneak at - tack. I

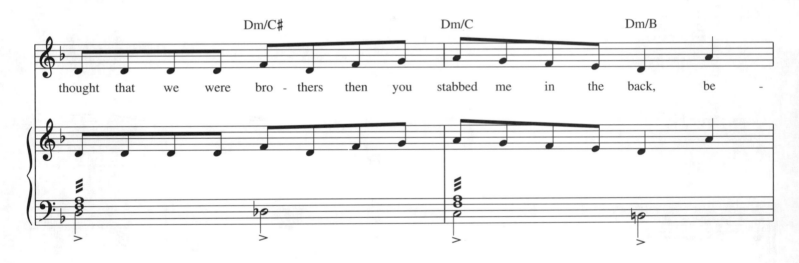

thought that we were bro - thers then you stabbed me in the back, be -

trayed. _____ Oh boy, I'm so be - trayed. Like

MAX: I'm drowning! I'm drowning here! I'm going down for the last time! I see my whole life flashing before my eyes!

(Spoken above the "bucolic" interlude)

MAX: I see a weathered old farmhouse, and a white picket fence. I'm running through fields of alfalfa with my collie, Rex. And I see my mother, standing on the back porch, in a worn but clean gingham gown, and I hear her calling out to me, "Alvin! Alvin! Don't forget your chores. The wood needs a cordin' and the cows need a milkin'. Alvin, Alvin..."

Bucolic, in 4

'TIL HIM

Music and Lyrics by
MEL BROOKS

Moderate Ballad

LEO: No one ev-er made me feel like some-one 'til him.

Life was real-ly noth-ing but a glum one 'til him.

My ex-ist-ence bor-dered on the trag-ic, al-ways tim-id, nev-er took a

PRISONERS OF LOVE
(Leo & Max)

Music and Lyrics by
MEL BROOKS

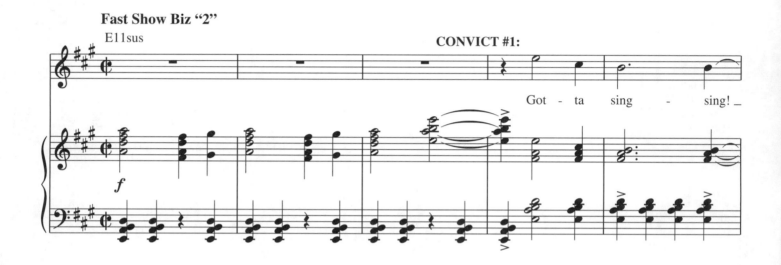

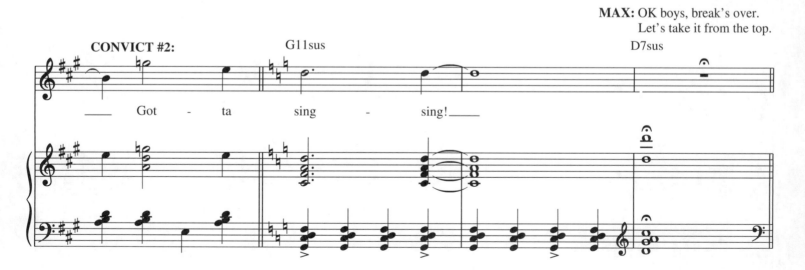

GOODBYE!

Music and Lyrics by
MEL BROOKS

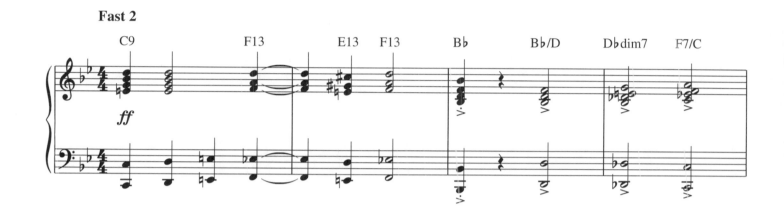

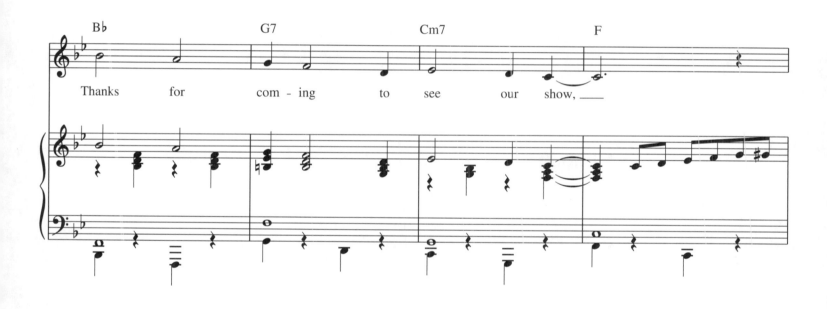

Thanks for com - ing to see our show, ___

sad to tell you we got to go. ___

THE ULTIMATE BROADWAY FAKE BOOK 4TH EDITION

Over 600 pages offering 725 songs from more than 200 Broadway shows! Recently revised to include hits from *Jekyll & Hyde, Martin Guerre, Rent, Sunset Boulevard, Victor/Victoria,* and more! This is the definitive collection of Broadway music, featuring: • Song title index • Show title index • Composer & lyricist index • Synopses of each show.

SONGS INCLUDE:

After You've Gone • Ain't Misbehavin' • All I Ask Of You • All Of You • All The Things You Are • Angel Of Music • Another Op'nin' Another Show • Another Suitcase In Another Hall • Any Dream Will Do • As If We Never Said Goodbye • As Long As He Needs Me • At The Ballet • Bali Ha'i • The Ballad Of Sweeney Todd • Beauty And The Beast • Beauty School Dropout • Bess, You Is My Woman • Bewitched • Blue Skies • Bring Him Home • Brotherhood Of Man • Buenos Aires • Cabaret • Camelot • Can't Help Lovin' Dat Man • Caravan • Castle On A Cloud • Comedy Tonight • Consider Yourself • Dance: Ten Looks: Three • Day By Day • Do I Hear A Waltz? • Do-Re-Mi • Do You Hear The People Sing? • Don't Cry For Me Argentina • Down In The Depths (On The Ninetieth Floor) • Easter Parade • Edelweiss • Everything's Coming Up Roses • Ev'ry Time We Say Goodbye • Getting To Know You • Give My Regards To Broadway • Guys And Dolls • Have You Met Miss Jones? • Heat Wave • Hello, Dolly! • Hey, Look Me Over • How Are Things In Glocca Morra • How High The Moon • I Can Dream, Can't I? • I Could Have Danced All Night • I Don't Know How To Love Him • I Dreamed A Dream • I Remember It Well • I Won't Grow Up • I've Grown Accustomed To Her Face • If Ever I Would Leave You • If I Can't Love Her • If I Were A Man • If I Were A Rich Man • (I'm A) Yankee Doodle Dandy • The Impossible Dream • It's The Hard-Knock Life • June Is Bustin' Out All Over • Kids! • La Cage Aux Folles • The Lady Is A Tramp • Lambeth Walk • Last Night Of The World • Let Me Entertain You • A Little Night Music • Living In The Shadows • Lost In The Stars • Love Changes Everything • Luck Be A Lady • Make Someone Happy • Makin' Whoopee! • Mame • Maria • Me And My Girl • Memory • Mood Indigo • The Music Of The Night • My Funny Valentine • My Heart Belongs To Daddy • A New Life • Oh, What A Beautiful Mornin' • Oklahoma • Ol' Man River • On A Clear Day (You Can See Forever) • On My Own • On Your Toes • One • One Night In Bangkok • Only You • Paris By Night • The Party's Over • People • People Will Say We're In Love • Phantom of the Opera • Quiet Night • The Rain In Spain • Satin Doll • Send In The Clowns • Seventy-Six Trombones • Shall We Dance? • Smoke Gets In Your Eyes • So In Love • Some Enchanted Evening • Someone • Someone Like You • The Sound Of Music • Standing On The Corner • Starlight Express • Summer Nights • Sun and Moon • Sunrise, Sunset • The Surrey With The Fringe On Top • Tell Me On A Sunday • Tell Me To Go • Thank Heaven For Little Girls • There's No Business Like Show Business • This Is The Moment • Tomorrow • Too Darn Hot • Tradition • Try To Remember • Unexpected Song • Waitin' For The Light To Shine • What I Did For Love • Wishing You Were Somehow Here Again • With One Look • You'll Never Walk Alone • and more!

00240046 . . . . **$39.95**

Price, contents, and availability subject to change without notice.